MY TRADITIONAL RECIPE JOURNAL

to record and preserve your
Family Recipe Secrets

ISBN: 978 1910853 269

published worldwide in 2020

Published by:

Lioness Publishing
LionessPublishing.com
facebook.com/LionessPublishing
twitter.com/lionesspublish

9 781910 853269

How to Use

MY TRADITIONAL

RECIPE JOURNAL

This recipe journal has been designed to help you to record, organise and preserve your favourite recipes. Whether they are your family recipe secrets handed down through the generations, your own personal creations, a personal twist on a family favourite, or trying out new ideas, you will find this recipe journal invaluable for recording your cooking creations.

The *Kitchen Conversions* section contains quick reference guides to help you convert US, Imperial and Metric weights and temperatures, plus a handy meat roasting guide lookup.

The *Contents* section provides an index for you to record the location of your recipes.

The *My Recipes* section is laid out for you to add your recipes, with plenty of space for ingredients and recording your cooking method.

The *Notes* section is a free form section for you to jot down things to remember, from that new brand of cheese you just tried, to that special ingredient from the farmer's market.

KITCHEN CONVERSIONS

Oven Temperatures

	Celsius	Fahrenheit	Gas Mark		Celsius	Fahrenheit	Gas Mark
Very Cool / Very Slow	110 C	225 F	¼	Moderate	190 C	375 F	5
Cool / Slow	120 C	250 F	½	Moderate / Hot	200 C	400 F	6
Warm	140 C	275 F	1	Moderate / Hot	210 C	410 F	6
Moderate	150 C	300 F	2	Hot	220 C	425 F	7
Moderate	160 C	325 F	3	Hot	230 C	450 F	8
Moderate	180 C	350 F	4	Hot	245 C	475 F	9

Dry Measures

Imperial	Metric	Imperial	Metric	Spoons	Metric
½ oz	15g	10oz	285g	¼ teaspoon	1ml
¾ oz	20g	11oz	310g	½ teaspoon	2.5ml
1oz	30g	12oz	340g	¾ teaspoon	4ml
2oz	60g	13oz	370g	1 teaspoon	5ml
3oz	85g	14oz	400g	1 dessertspoon	10ml
4oz	115g	15oz	425g	1 tablespoon	15ml
5oz	140g	16oz	450g		
6oz	170g	24oz	680g		
7oz	200g	32oz	0.9kg		
8oz	230g	48oz	1.4kg		
9oz	255g	64oz	1.8kg		

Liquid Measures

Pints	Metric	Cups	Fl. Oz.
-	100ml	-	3 ½
-	125ml	½	4 ½
¼	150ml	-	5
-	200ml	-	7
-	250nl	1	9
½	275ml	-	10
-	300nl	-	11
-	400ml	-	14
-	500ml	2	18
1	570ml	-	20
-	750ml	3	26
1 ¾	1.0 L	4	35
2	1.1 L	-	40
-	1.3 L	5	46
3	1.7 L	-	60
-	2.0 L	8	70

Roasting Guide

Meat	Preheat Oven	Roast Time	Oven Temp	Roast Time	Resting Time
Beef / Lamb / Venison < 5Kg/11lb RARE	220 C 435 F GM 7	30 mins	180 C 350 F GM 4-5	20 mins / ½ kg 9 mins / lb	20 – 30 mins
Beef / Lamb / Venison < 5Kg/11lb MEDIUM	220 C 435 F GM 7	30 mins	180 C 350 F GM 4-5	30 mins / ½ kg 14 mins / lb	20 – 30 mins
Beef / Lamb / Venison < 5Kg/11lb WELL DONE	220 C 435 F GM 7	30 mins	180 C 350 F GM 4-5	40 mins / ½ kg 18 mins / lb	20 – 30 mins
Pork MEDIUM	220 C 425 F GM 7	30 mins	180 C 350 F GM 3	30 mins / ½ kg 23 mins / lb	20 – 30 mins
Pork WELL DONE	220 C 425 F GM 7	35 mins	180 C 350 F GM 4	35 mins / ½ kg 16 mins / lb	20 – 30 mins
Chicken	210 C 435 F GM 6	20 mins	180 C 350 F GM 4	45 mins / small 70 mins / large	20 mins
Turkey	220 C 450 F GM 7	20 mins	180 C 350 F GM 4	100 mins / small 200 mins / large	20 - 30 mins
Goose	220 C 425 F GM 7	20 mins	180 C 350 F GM 4	70 – 120 mins	20 - 30 mins
Duck	220 C 425 F GM 7	20 mins	180 C 350 F GM 4	35 – 45 mins	10 mins

CONTENTS

Page	Recipe Title

Page   Recipe Title

Page   Recipe Title

_____

_____

_____

_____

_____

_____

_____

_____

_____

_____

_____

_____

_____

_____

Page	Recipe Title

MY RECIPES

RECIPE:

Prep Time: Oven Temp: Cooking Time:

Difficulty:

_____

Easy - Medium - Hard

INGREDIENTS

SERVES: _____

_____
_____
_____
_____
_____
_____
_____
_____
_____
_____
_____
_____
_____
_____

_____
_____
_____
_____
_____
_____
_____
_____
_____
_____
_____
_____
_____
_____

Method

_____
_____
_____
_____
_____
_____
_____
_____
_____
_____
_____
_____
_____
_____
_____
_____
_____
_____
_____
_____
_____

RECIPE:

Prep Time: Oven Temp: Cooking Time:

Difficulty:

Easy - Medium - Hard

INGREDIENTS

SERVES:

Method

RECIPE:

Prep Time: Oven Temp: Cooking Time: Difficulty:

_____   Easy - Medium - Hard

INGREDIENTS   SERVES: _____

_____   _____
_____   _____
_____   _____
_____   _____

_____   _____
_____   _____
_____   _____
_____   _____

_____   _____
_____   _____
_____   _____
_____   _____

Method

RECIPE:

Prep Time: Oven Temp: Cooking Time:

Difficulty:

_____

Easy - Medium - Hard

INGREDIENTS

SERVES: _____

_____ _____
_____ _____
_____ _____
_____ _____
_____ _____
_____ _____
_____ _____
_____ _____
_____ _____
_____ _____
_____ _____
_____ _____

Method

RECIPE:

Prep Time: Oven Temp: Cooking Time:

_____

Difficulty:

Easy - Medium - Hard

INGREDIENTS

SERVES: _____

_____ _____
_____ _____
_____ _____
_____ _____
_____ _____

_____ _____
_____ _____
_____ _____
_____ _____

_____ _____
_____ _____
_____ _____
_____ _____

Method

RECIPE:

Prep Time: Oven Temp: Cooking Time:

Difficulty:

Easy - Medium - Hard

INGREDIENTS

SERVES:

Method

RECIPE:

Prep Time: Oven Temp: Cooking Time:

_____

INGREDIENTS

_____

_____

_____

_____

_____

_____

_____

_____

_____

_____

_____

_____

Difficulty:

Easy - Medium - Hard

SERVES: _____

_____

_____

_____

_____

_____

_____

_____

_____

_____

_____

_____

_____

Method

_____

_____

_____

_____

_____

_____

_____

_____

_____

_____

_____

_____

_____

_____

_____

_____

_____

_____

_____

RECIPE:

Prep Time: Oven Temp: Cooking Time: Difficulty:

_____ _____   Easy - Medium - Hard

INGREDIENTS   SERVES: _____

_____   _____
_____   _____
_____   _____
_____   _____
_____   _____

_____   _____
_____   _____
_____   _____

_____   _____
_____   _____
_____   _____
_____   _____

Method

RECIPE:

Prep Time: Oven Temp: Cooking Time:

Difficulty:

Easy - Medium - Hard

INGREDIENTS

SERVES: _____

Method

RECIPE:

Prep Time: Oven Temp: Cooking Time:

Difficulty:

_____

Easy - Medium - Hard

INGREDIENTS

SERVES: _____

_____   _____
_____   _____
_____   _____
_____   _____

_____   _____
_____   _____
_____   _____

_____   _____
_____   _____
_____   _____

_____   _____
_____   _____

Method

RECIPE:

Prep Time: Oven Temp: Cooking Time:

Difficulty:

Easy - Medium - Hard

INGREDIENTS

SERVES:

Method

RECIPE:

Prep Time: Oven Temp: Cooking Time:

Difficulty:

Easy - Medium - Hard

INGREDIENTS

SERVES:

_____   _____
_____   _____
_____   _____
_____   _____
_____   _____
_____   _____
_____   _____
_____   _____
_____   _____
_____   _____
_____   _____
_____   _____
_____   _____
_____   _____

Method

RECIPE:

Prep Time: Oven Temp: Cooking Time:

Difficulty:

Easy - Medium - Hard

INGREDIENTS

SERVES: _____

_____   _____
_____   _____
_____   _____
_____   _____

_____   _____
_____   _____
_____   _____
_____   _____

_____   _____
_____   _____
_____   _____
_____   _____

Method

RECIPE:

Prep Time: Oven Temp: Cooking Time: Difficulty:

_____   Easy - Medium - Hard

INGREDIENTS   SERVES: _____

_____   _____
_____   _____
_____   _____
_____   _____

_____   _____
_____   _____
_____   _____

_____   _____
_____   _____
_____   _____

_____   _____
_____   _____
_____   _____

Method

RECIPE:

Prep Time: Oven Temp: Cooking Time: Difficulty:

_____   Easy - Medium - Hard

INGREDIENTS   SERVES: _____

_____   _____
_____   _____
_____   _____
_____   _____

_____   _____
_____   _____
_____   _____
_____   _____
_____   _____
_____   _____
_____   _____

Method

RECIPE:

Prep Time: Oven Temp: Cooking Time:

Difficulty:

Easy - Medium - Hard

INGREDIENTS

SERVES:

Method

RECIPE:

Prep Time: Oven Temp: Cooking Time:

Difficulty:

_____

Easy - Medium - Hard

INGREDIENTS

SERVES: _____

_____   _____

_____   _____

_____   _____

_____   _____

_____   _____

_____   _____

_____   _____

_____   _____

_____   _____

_____   _____

_____   _____

_____   _____

_____   _____

Method

RECIPE:

Prep Time: Oven Temp: Cooking Time:

Difficulty:

_____

Easy - Medium - Hard

INGREDIENTS

SERVES: _____

_____   _____
_____   _____
_____   _____
_____   _____

_____   _____
_____   _____
_____   _____

_____   _____
_____   _____
_____   _____

_____   _____
_____   _____
_____   _____

Method

RECIPE:

Prep Time: Oven Temp: Cooking Time:

_____

INGREDIENTS

_____

_____

_____

_____

_____

_____

_____

_____

_____

_____

_____

_____

Difficulty:

Easy - Medium - Hard

SERVES: _____

_____

_____

_____

_____

_____

_____

_____

_____

_____

_____

_____

_____

Method

RECIPE:

Prep Time: Oven Temp: Cooking Time:

Difficulty:

Easy - Medium - Hard

INGREDIENTS

SERVES:

Method

RECIPE:

Prep Time: Oven Temp: Cooking Time:

Difficulty:

Easy - Medium - Hard

INGREDIENTS

SERVES: _____

Method

RECIPE:

Prep Time: Oven Temp: Cooking Time:

Difficulty:

Easy - Medium - Hard

INGREDIENTS

SERVES:

_____

_____

_____

_____

_____

_____

_____

_____

_____

_____

_____

_____

_____

_____

_____

_____

_____

_____

_____

_____

_____

_____

_____

_____

_____

_____

Method

RECIPE:

Prep Time: Oven Temp: Cooking Time:

Difficulty:

Easy - Medium - Hard

INGREDIENTS

SERVES: _____

_____   _____

_____   _____

_____   _____

_____   _____

_____   _____

_____   _____

_____   _____

_____   _____

_____   _____

_____   _____

_____   _____

_____   _____

Method

RECIPE:

Prep Time: Oven Temp: Cooking Time:

Difficulty:

Easy - Medium - Hard

INGREDIENTS

SERVES:

_____   _____
_____   _____
_____   _____
_____   _____

_____   _____
_____   _____
_____   _____
_____   _____
_____   _____
_____   _____
_____   _____
_____   _____
_____   _____

Method

RECIPE:

Prep Time: Oven Temp: Cooking Time:

Difficulty:

Easy - Medium - Hard

INGREDIENTS

SERVES: _____

Method

RECIPE:

Prep Time: Oven Temp: Cooking Time:

_____

Difficulty:

Easy - Medium - Hard

INGREDIENTS

SERVES: _____

_____
_____
_____
_____

_____
_____
_____

_____
_____
_____
_____
_____

_____
_____
_____
_____
_____
_____
_____
_____

_____
_____
_____
_____
_____
_____
_____
_____

Method

RECIPE:

Prep Time: Oven Temp: Cooking Time:

Difficulty:

Easy - Medium - Hard

INGREDIENTS

SERVES:

_____   _____
_____   _____
_____   _____
_____   _____
_____   _____
_____   _____
_____   _____
_____   _____
_____   _____
_____   _____
_____   _____
_____   _____
_____   _____

Method

_____

_____

_____

_____

_____

_____

_____

_____

_____

_____

_____

_____

_____

_____

_____

_____

_____

_____

_____

_____

_____

RECIPE:

Prep Time: Oven Temp: Cooking Time: Difficulty:

_____   Easy - Medium - Hard

INGREDIENTS   SERVES: _____

_____   _____

_____   _____

_____   _____

_____   _____

_____   _____

_____   _____

_____   _____

_____   _____

_____   _____

_____   _____

_____   _____

_____   _____

Method

RECIPE:

Prep Time: Oven Temp: Cooking Time:

Difficulty:

Easy - Medium - Hard

INGREDIENTS

SERVES:

Method

RECIPE:

Prep Time: Oven Temp: Cooking Time:

Difficulty:

Easy - Medium - Hard

INGREDIENTS

SERVES: _____

_____   _____
_____   _____
_____   _____
_____   _____
_____   _____
_____   _____
_____   _____
_____   _____
_____   _____
_____   _____
_____   _____
_____   _____
_____   _____
_____   _____

Method

RECIPE:

Prep Time: Oven Temp: Cooking Time: Difficulty:

_____   _____   _____   Easy - Medium - Hard

INGREDIENTS   SERVES: _____

_____   _____
_____   _____
_____   _____
_____   _____

_____   _____
_____   _____
_____   _____
_____   _____
_____   _____
_____   _____
_____   _____

Method

RECIPE:

Prep Time: Oven Temp: Cooking Time:

Difficulty:

_____

Easy - Medium - Hard

INGREDIENTS

SERVES: _____

_____   _____
_____   _____
_____   _____
_____   _____

_____   _____
_____   _____
_____   _____
_____   _____
_____   _____
_____   _____
_____   _____
_____   _____

Method

RECIPE:

Prep Time: Oven Temp: Cooking Time:

Difficulty:

Easy - Medium - Hard

INGREDIENTS

SERVES: _____

_____   _____
_____   _____
_____   _____
_____   _____
_____   _____
_____   _____
_____   _____
_____   _____
_____   _____
_____   _____
_____   _____
_____   _____
_____   _____

Method

RECIPE:

Prep Time: Oven Temp: Cooking Time:

_____

INGREDIENTS

_____

_____

_____

_____

_____

_____

_____

_____

_____

_____

_____

_____

_____

Difficulty:

Easy - Medium - Hard

SERVES: _____

_____

_____

_____

_____

_____

_____

_____

_____

_____

_____

_____

_____

_____

Method

RECIPE:

Prep Time: Oven Temp: Cooking Time:

Difficulty:

Easy - Medium - Hard

INGREDIENTS

SERVES: _____

Method

RECIPE:

Prep Time: Oven Temp: Cooking Time:

Difficulty:

_____   _____   _____

Easy - Medium - Hard

INGREDIENTS

SERVES: _____

_____   _____
_____   _____
_____   _____
_____   _____
_____   _____
_____   _____
_____   _____
_____   _____
_____   _____
_____   _____
_____   _____
_____   _____
_____   _____
_____   _____
_____   _____

Method

RECIPE:

Prep Time: Oven Temp: Cooking Time:

Difficulty:

Easy - Medium - Hard

INGREDIENTS

SERVES: _____

_____   _____
_____   _____
_____   _____
_____   _____
_____   _____
_____   _____
_____   _____
_____   _____
_____   _____
_____   _____
_____   _____
_____   _____
_____   _____
_____   _____

Method

RECIPE:

Prep Time: Oven Temp: Cooking Time: Difficulty:

_____   Easy - Medium - Hard

INGREDIENTS   SERVES: _____

_____   _____

_____   _____

_____   _____

_____   _____

_____   _____

_____   _____

_____   _____

_____   _____

_____   _____

_____   _____

_____   _____

Method

RECIPE:

Prep Time: Oven Temp: Cooking Time:

Difficulty:

Easy - Medium - Hard

INGREDIENTS

SERVES: _____

Method

RECIPE:

Prep Time: Oven Temp: Cooking Time:

Difficulty:

Easy - Medium - Hard

INGREDIENTS

SERVES:

Method

RECIPE:

Prep Time: Oven Temp: Cooking Time:

Difficulty:

Easy - Medium - Hard

INGREDIENTS

SERVES: _____

_____ _____
_____ _____
_____ _____
_____ _____

_____ _____
_____ _____
_____ _____
_____ _____
_____ _____
_____ _____
_____ _____

Method

RECIPE:

Prep Time: Oven Temp: Cooking Time:

Difficulty:

Easy - Medium - Hard

INGREDIENTS

SERVES: _____

Method

RECIPE:

Prep Time: Oven Temp: Cooking Time:

Difficulty:

_____

Easy - Medium - Hard

INGREDIENTS

SERVES: _____

_____   _____
_____   _____
_____   _____
_____   _____
_____   _____
_____   _____
_____   _____
_____   _____
_____   _____
_____   _____
_____   _____
_____   _____

Method

RECIPE:

Prep Time: Oven Temp: Cooking Time:

Difficulty:

_____

Easy - Medium - Hard

INGREDIENTS

SERVES: _____

_____   _____
_____   _____
_____   _____
_____   _____

_____   _____
_____   _____
_____   _____
_____   _____
_____   _____
_____   _____
_____   _____
_____   _____
_____   _____

Method

RECIPE:

Prep Time: Oven Temp: Cooking Time:

Difficulty:

_____

Easy - Medium - Hard

INGREDIENTS

SERVES: _____

_____   _____
_____   _____
_____   _____
_____   _____

_____   _____
_____   _____
_____   _____
_____   _____
_____   _____
_____   _____
_____   _____
_____   _____

Method

RECIPE:

Prep Time: Oven Temp: Cooking Time:

Difficulty:

Easy - Medium - Hard

INGREDIENTS

SERVES:

Method

RECIPE:

Prep Time: Oven Temp: Cooking Time:

INGREDIENTS

Difficulty:

Easy - Medium - Hard

SERVES:

Method

RECIPE:

Prep Time: Oven Temp: Cooking Time:

Difficulty:

Easy - Medium - Hard

INGREDIENTS

SERVES:

Method

RECIPE:

Prep Time: Oven Temp: Cooking Time:

Difficulty:

Easy - Medium - Hard

INGREDIENTS

SERVES: _____

Method

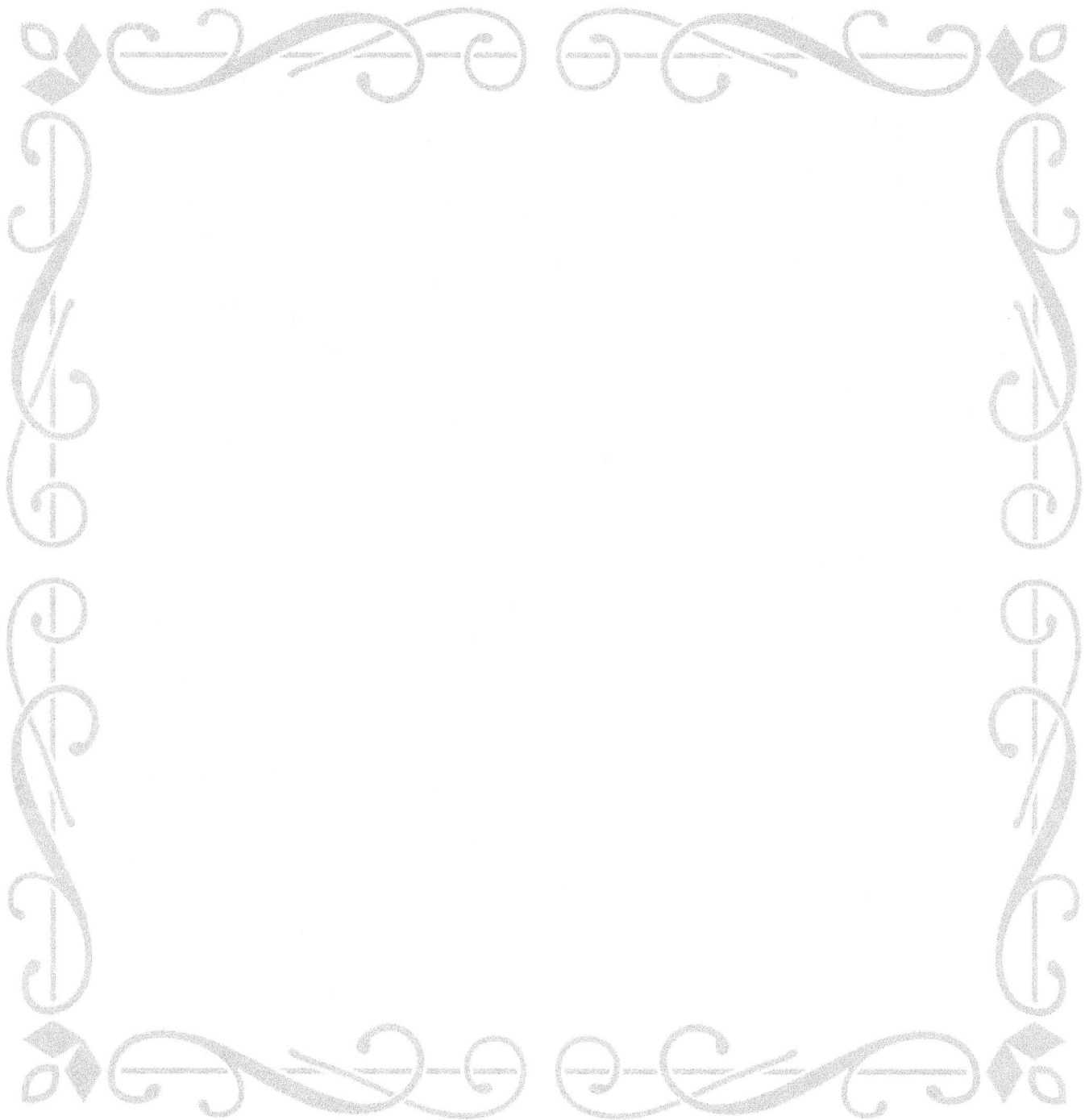

MY NOTES

Notes

Notes

Notes

Notes

Notes

Notes

Notes

Notes

Notes

Notes

Notes

Notes

Notes

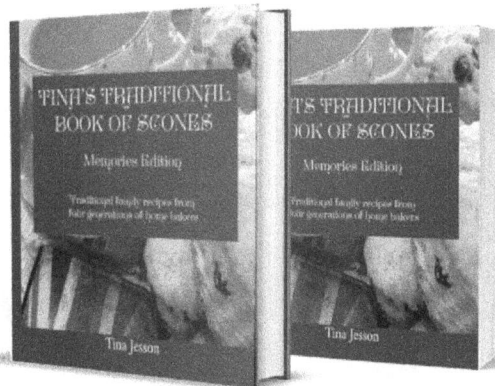

PUBLISH YOUR FAMILY RECIPES

Publishing your family recipe secrets will preserve your treasured recipes through the generations.

After you have collected and recorded your family recipes, why not get them professionally published with a glossy cover, in hardback or paperback.

A priceless memento for you, a wonderful gift for your family.

Publish privately, or make it available worldwide.

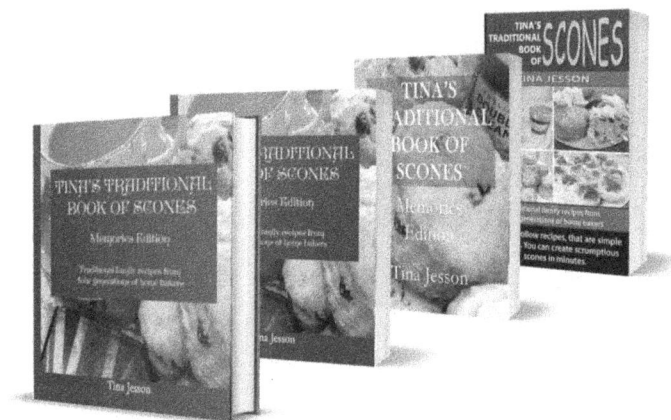

FIND OUT MORE: LionessPublishing.com/my-family-recipes

www.ingramcontent.com/pod-product-compliance
Lightning Source LLC
Chambersburg PA
CBHW050639150426

42813CB00054B/1123